MW01242485

THE ESTONIAN SPY

A True Story of Resistance to Russian Oppression

Reinolt Tönis Tofer

Ken Hallenbeck

TerraPrime Publications
A division of TerraPrime, LLC
www.terraprime.org

First Edition

CONTENTS

Preface

This book is a collection of stories of an Estonian man named Tom Saar. He was born in 1934 in Estonia and was forced to flee with his family when Russia invaded the country during WWII. He survived as a refugee in Sweden and eventually volunteered to serve in the United States Army 10th Special Forces Group during the Cold War, motivated by a need to avenge his home country for its brutal treatment by the Red Army.

In the United States, much has been written about the impact of World War II on countries like Britain, Germany, Poland, Russia, and Japan, but there is less attention given to the smaller countries whose societies and peoples were turned upside-down by the war and its outcome. Estonia, a small Baltic country that shares its eastern border with Russia, was one such country. Estonia resisted Russian influence for decades leading up to WWII, only to be turned over to Russia and become part of the USSR. It finally re-established independence in 1991.

80 years after its 1941 invasion of Estonia, Russia is again threatening the sovereignty of its neighbors. Tom's stories illustrate the personal impact these wars of aggression have on the lives of individual people caught up in the conflict. They are about the past - but in them we can find a glimpse of the fate waiting for the children displaced by today's wars. They span the first three decades of Tom's life, and are based on eyewitness interviews conducted in 2022 and 2023.

We are fortunate to have acquired a collection of images depicting the people and places in Tom's stories. They are included throughout the main text and in the appendix. For privacy reasons, some names, dates, and locations may have been changed.

Prologue

On May 1st, 1958, I boarded a train in West Berlin. Instead of my uniform, I was dressed in civilian clothes in order to blend in with my fellow passengers. It was strictly against policy to go on counter-espionage missions alone, but I couldn't bear to let the Russians operate unchecked, spewing their communist propaganda in Allied-held territory. I had seen first-hand what their lies could do to a country. I had seen it tear my homeland apart. And when I joined the U.S. Army, I swore to get revenge for all the suffering the Red Army had caused my family. So there I was, sitting alone, staring at the cityscape as the train slowly began to move out of the station toward Mannheim, Germany.

The threat in Mannheim was undefined. Like most of my missions as part of the newly-formed 10th Special Forces Group, or 10th SFG, word had come as whispers from informants in East Berlin. All I knew was that there would be "Russian activity" in several Allied-held factory towns on Labour Day. Alone, I would have to limit my mission to reconnaissance and report back to Berlin on anything out of the ordinary. I stared at my lap, noticing how tightly clasped my hands were, and tried to quell the anger burning in my chest. I hated the Russians and the poisonous words they were spreading. I also knew I shouldn't try to disrupt them while operating alone: doing so would endanger both my mission and myself. But I wanted to. The idea of observation - that is to say, inaction - frustrated me.

I looked up at the window and found that the city had disappeared. The rolling green hills of the countryside were sliding past, covered with late spring flowers. It was nice to get out of the city for a little while. As the train rolled past a lowland meadow, I saw a few spotted-orchids, purple and white, just like the ones that bloomed in the summers in Estonia. My anger started to ebb. I would do my duty. My civilian clothes would enable me to slip through the Soviet checkpoints on the way out of East Germany. Once in Mannheim, I would observe, identify, and report back.

The train slowed down as it approached the Mannheim station and eventually squealed to a stop. I disembarked along with a handful of other passengers. As I exited the station, I could hear shouting, and saw a large crowd gathered in the town center not far away. I picked up my pace, boots landing heavily on the cobblestone street as I walked full-stride toward the din. Even before I could make out the words among the noise, I knew this had to be the "Russian activity" I had been sent to observe. Over the heads of the crowd I could make out two figures standing on boxes in front of the large stone form of the Mannheim Water Tower. Shoving my hands into my pockets, I slowed to a casual stroll, doing my best to look mildly curious. As I joined the fringes of the crowd, a gathering of 100-or-so, I found that the noise was actually coming almost entirely from the men standing on the boxes. They were taking turns shouting about the many failures of capitalism while the crowd stood and watched silently. I rolled my eyes despite myself. The Russians really had lost all sense of subtly. Mannheim was hundreds of miles into Allied territory, and it was likely the spectacle of two fellows shouting in the city center which had attracted the crowd, rather than any sympathy the townsfolk had for communism.

I watched the Russians - it was obvious that these were the Russian agents here to disrupt factory work, even if they didn't look or sound Russian - and the crowd for about 10 minutes. The gathering wasn't growing, which was good. But it wasn't shrinking either. My lips tightened into a thin line. How could these people just stand here, quietly listening to this garbage? I knew they hadn't experienced the horrors behind the words. They had experienced different horrors during the war, but they hadn't experienced a Russian occupation. Not yet, at least. Hopefully, they never would - that was why I was here in the first place. I *had* experienced it first-hand. I felt my resolve to remain silent slipping away as anger crept back into my chest. Thinking back to my childhood had been a mistake.

The taller of the two communist preachers was a talented orator. The fellow spoke with the kind of energy that caught the eye and the mind even if the words were lies. It was the same old propaganda, cycling though the gripes of long hours, low wages, and competing against your neighbor. His pace accelerated as he tried to energize the crowd. In response, the crowd had started to hum with the kind of side conversations that meant he may have lost their attention instead. Then, someone shouted a response directly back at him, jeering rather than sympathizing. I looked around and assessed the situation, which seemed to be at a turning point. There were only two Russians. Perhaps I could subtly disperse the crowd? The group seemed to be on my side, and with other people finally starting to shout back, I could risk a comment or two just to help steer things in the right direction. I focused back on the Russian up front.

"How long must we continue to work for a pittance that can barely feed our families??" The shorter Russian was shouting. "Where is the dignity in laboring to survi-"

"At least we have jobs!" I shouted back, with a bit more heat than intended. There was a loud shuffling of feet and craning of necks as those near me turned to get a look at the new challenger. If the Russian was surprised by the interruption, he didn't show it.

"Jobs handed out to you by a capitalist who lives across the ocean! What kind of life is that? Building wealth not for yourself or your country but for an American!" Some of the people in the crowd grumbled in agreement, and my anger spiked.

"America is rebuilding Germany, not exploiting her!" As soon as I said it, I knew I had chosen the wrong words. It was never a good idea to use the word "exploit" in a country as heavily occupied as post-war Germany. Even though I felt strongly that the American efforts to rebuild the country were going well, the people around me wouldn't necessarily agree, especially with a sentiment stated so strongly. My fears were confirmed by my neighbors, who shifted uncomfortably and looked away. I gritted my teeth. I had let my anger get the better of me. Then I caught movement out of the corner of my eye. Two men were shouldering their way through the crowd toward me. Apparently the two speakers weren't the only Russians in Mannheim - a second miscalculation. My comments had made me a target. It was time to leave.

I backed out of the throng as quickly as I could. I had resolved to do nothing, but I had failed. Now, all that mattered was getting back safely so I could report what I had observed. I had gotten a good look at the two fellows speaking and would sketch their faces for a new investigation file after I returned to Berlin.

Once I was free of the crowd I started to walk quickly toward the train station. Perhaps they weren't after me, but the other crowd member who had shouted back? After a few moments I looked back over my shoulder, and watched two men break free of the crowd, only twenty paces behind. Shit! I broke into a run and hurtled down the main street as fast as I could. I eyed each side street as I sprinted, hoping for a place to shake my pursuers. A glance backward confirmed I was losing them - the endless physical training of the 10th SFG was paying off. Three streets down I found the perfect alley and ducked in, still running at full-speed. Two quick turns later, I stumbled to a halt on an out-of-the-way road and bent over to catch my breath. My lungs burned and I could feel my heart beating nearly out of my chest, but the adrenaline kept the rest of my exertion relegated to my subconscious. From where I had stopped, I could barely hear the clamor of the main street.

Looking around to get my bearings, I found myself surrounded by images of scantily-clad women plastered on nearly every door and window. I chuckled. No mystery here: I had sprinted into the Red Light district. That explained why this causeway was so quiet - at this time of day, at least. In a few windows, curious and heavily made-up faces peered out at the strange man wheezing on their sidewalk. I waved faintly.

Then the sounds of heavy boots pounding the pavement came from behind, and I threw myself back into a dead sprint. Right as I was about to round a corner back toward the main street, one of the Russians turned the corner from the other side, coming right at me. There was no time to react. We collided and collapsed into a heap.

I struggled back to my feet and turned to run, but it was no good. The second Russian had caught up and kicked me in the ribs, sending me crashing back down to the pavement. My whole body exploded in pain, and my mind raced. I had to find a way - any way - out of this situation. I staggered to my feet and tried to shuffle back toward the nearest building to protect myself, but the Russians advanced toward me. The street was empty except for my assailants. I tried to throw a defensive kick as they reached me, but they swatted my leg aside and began to kick every exposed part of me. Each glance or lunge toward an exit was met with another blow.

A full minute passed as the Russians pummeled me. Then another. It felt like an eternity, stretching onward in an endless stream of blows and yet somehow each new strike seemed to hurt less than the last. My body started to go numb, and I realized with a strange calmness that this was it. They weren't going to stop beating me until I was dead. They knew I was an American operative and they were going to kill me.

Suddenly, a woman's scream pierced the air from somewhere behind them. As the Russians turned, the door next to me cracked open and a hand shot out to pull me in. With all the strength I had left, I lunged toward the opening and scrambled inside. The woman who had saved me slammed the windowless door shut and bolted it twice. I lay on the floor, bruised, bleeding, and gasping for air, listening to the Russians beat on the entryway and swear death upon the inhabitants. Fortunately, the brothel took its locks seriously. The door didn't budge. After a few minutes, the yelling from outside subsided - the Russians likely knew the local police were on the way. I rested my head on the cold wood of the floor, and breathed a long, painful sigh of relief. I recall looking around at the dimly lit entryway of the German brothel and almost managing a laugh. What strange turns of fate had brought me here?

Map of Northern Europe, noting locations from Tom's stories.

CHAPTER 1

Estonia

My name is Tom Saar. I was born to Heino and Leida
Saar in 1934 at Tallinn City Hospital, in the capital of Estonia.
My father, Heino, was the son of an influential businessman.
Grandpa had political connections that ran up to the highest
levels of the Estonian government. This provided both social
and monetary wealth to my family, and as a result the Saars
filled a variety of important government roles in the 1920s and
1930s. My grandfather's brother served as the first Estonian
ambassador to Italy, Germany and Russia before I was born.
My aunt Magarethe, or Grete as we called her, was married to
the *Kaitseminister,* the man in charge of the *Kaitseministeerium*
(the Estonian Ministry of Defense). My father also did well for
himself: he operated an extremely successful textile factory in
Tallinn, which funded a comfortable life on an expansive
family farm in Vasalemma, 40 km south of Tallinn.

This family farm, called Uuemõisa, is where my earliest
memories are. There, my father and my two uncles, Paul and
Fritz, raised hundreds of cattle and dozens of horses and other
livestock as part of the family's business. I loved the horses
most of all. Even as a four-year-old I had begun to stomp
around the muddy barn learning to care for them and how to
ride them.

My grandmother, who hoped to prepare me for a life of
international business, hired a governess for me at the age of 3
who only spoke to me in German. I called her "Tata".
Generally, I preferred to speak in my native Estonian, but Tata
had such wonderful stories of her previous service in St.

Petersburg at the Tsar's palace that I was happy to learn German to hear more. She had fled the communist takeover of Russia and found employment with the Saar family.

My happy world on the family farm ended abruptly when I was 5 years old. On August 23rd, 1939, Germany and the Soviet Union stunned the world with the signing of a Non-Aggression Pact called the Molotov-Ribbentrop agreement. On its face, the pact was a peace deal between the two countries, including arbitration over conflicts, and neutrality in case of war with a third party. I was too young to understand what this meant for Estonia, but I can remember how much anxiety and concern the announcement caused my parents. When Germany's invasion of Poland kicked off World War II less than two weeks later, there was little else they wanted to do but gather around the radio to hear the latest dreadful news. All of Estonia was holding its breath, waiting and listening to the progress of the German war in Poland, and wondering whether the hammer of war would fall on us as well.

What my parents, the Estonia government, and the broader world didn't realize was that the Molotov-Ribbentrop agreement carried confidential terms dictating spheres of influence for Germany and the Soviet Union. It defined which European nations each would control. Germany would occupy Western Poland, East Prussia and Lithuania while the USSR would control Finland, Eastern Poland, Latvia, and, most importantly for us, Estonia. These confidential terms, called the Secret Protocol, wouldn't be made known to the rest of the world until the Nuremberg trials 15 years later. However, when the USSR invaded Poland from the east on September 17th, 16 days after the German invasion from the west, we knew for certain that our country was caught, inextricably, between the hooked cross and the hammer and sickle.

The leaders of our small country felt that war with Russia should be avoided at all costs. Accordingly, Estonia declared itself a neutral party after the outbreak of the war.

Russia ignored the declaration, and during the month that followed, began to move their army and navy into Estonia. Soon, we started seeing Russian bombers fly patrols over Tallinn, and it became a regular occurrence to wake up during the night to the sound of planes flying overhead. By the 24th of September, our ports were blocked by Red Army warships. Russia demanded, with all its military might at the ready, to be allowed to establish military bases, move troops throughout the country and to have free use of Tallinn's port. In an effort to buy peace, the Estonian government conceded, and on September 28th, our leaders signed the mutual assistance agreement that had been forced on them. Russia moved in.

The following year was tense, but things continued relatively normally until June. On June 14, 1940, while the attention of the western world was caught up by the fall of Paris to the Nazis, Russia began conquering Estonia. With little hope of repelling invaders who were already stationed throughout the country, the Estonian government mounted no resistance. By June 16, the Soviet Union takeover of Estonia was complete. So, at 5-years old, I found myself living in a Soviet-controlled country. Despite my family's political connections, including the fact that my great-uncle had personally met both Stalin and Hitler during his time as an Estonian Ambassador, my family gained no protection from the rapid changes that soon began.

At first, the Red Army leadership that took over administration of Tallinn told my father, Heino, to stay and continue running the family textile factory. Even I, young as I was, could tell that he was uneasy. There were rumors that the Russians were rounding up and imprisoning all Estonians who had any political clout. Our family, not being directly involved with Estonian politics at the time, was far enough removed that we thought we might avoid the same fate - but it was hard to know. At first, my father decided to stay and continue running the textile business. Everything seemed fine for about a week. But one morning, when he arrived at the factory, there were

Soviet guards posted outside. My father hadn't asked for additional security, and when he asked after their orders, the guard rebuffed him. He worked uneasily for a few days with the guards stationed outside, but the following week brought more changes. Two Russians with rifles joined the regular crew. These men matter-of-factly sat my father down and forced him to sign a document nationalizing the factory."This is Russia now," they insisted. "You are Russian now, so this is Russia's factory".

I remember that day vividly. My father came home and immediately began planning for us to leave Estonia. He called on the family's diplomatic connections and secured German passports for us all. Later, I learned that choosing German passports had been strategic, and served a dual purpose. We would need documents to travel, but also, under the Secret Protocol of the Molotov-Ribbentrop agreement, Germans who owned land or business in the Soviet sphere of influence were to be compensated for the nationalization of their assets. Our family factory and farm were to be nationalized by Russia, and if my father could show documents proving he was German, he would qualify for the compensation. With this one act he both set up our emigration from our Soviet-occupied home and funded our move abroad. We stayed long enough to receive Stalin's payoff, then boarded a train for Germany.

My parents and I, along with my grandmother and my two uncles, Paul and Fritz, all traveled together. We were far from the only folk fleeing the country. The train was crowded with around 50 Germans and Estonians, all hoping to travel from Tallinn through Latvia, Lithuania and Poland, to Nuremberg, Germany. The 10 hour journey was tense. It would have been much shorter, but passenger documents were checked at each border crossing, so every few hours a wave of uniformed men with suspicious eyes would walk up and down the train, interrogating each family while looking through their papers. Thankfully, my father had acquired the German citizenship documents for us all and our family passed through the southern Baltic states without incident.

When we arrived in Germany, I expected a refugee camp. My parents had spoken highly of the country, but the chaos of the war and the flight had made me fear we'd be living in a barn like the horses back at home. Instead, we were moved into what I can only describe as a mansion. It was the private residence of a wealthy German family, and it was well-positioned in the countryside near Feucht, a small town outside Nuremberg. My family boarded together in a spacious room filled with furniture more elegant than the finishings in our own home.

Our departure from Estonia had come not a moment too soon. Shortly after we fled, the Soviet Union set up elections that were rigged to install Russian sympathizers into nearly all government leadership roles. Then began a brutal campaign of repression. More than 8000 Estonians in government service and public positions were arrested. They were then either executed or deported to hard labor camps in Siberia, from which few ever returned. The intention of the occupiers seemed to be a total dismantling of the Estonia political class, and the goal was achieved in less than a year.

We stayed through the German winter at the countryside mansion in Feucht. I celebrated my 6th birthday and enrolled in my first year of school, though it came amidst an uncertain future as a refugee. Thanks to Tata, I already spoke and understood German, so even while everything else in our lives was in upheaval, I adjusted to schooling in Germany rather well. After the school year ended in the spring of 1941, we were not permitted to stay a second year in Feucht. Thus, my whole family moved to more permanent accommodations in Berlin, almost 300 miles to the north. We moved to Berlin with the intention of staying there only as long as necessary. My parents and many other Estonians hoped pressure from neighboring countries or resistance from within Estonia might destabilize the Russian occupation and allow them to return. News had traveled of a guerilla force known as the "*metsavennad*", or Forest Brothers, that had formed within Estonia to protect innocent civilians. My uncles Paul and Fritz talked endlessly over the kitchen table about sneaking back to join the resistance. But it was merely talk, and there was no sign of a safe return being possible anytime soon. Russia was still in control.

On June 22, 1941, Germany reneged on the Non-Aggression Pact, turned on its Soviet partners, and began a east-ward invasion of Poland. In response, Stalin announced a scorched-earth policy that would have dire consequences for my homeland. Russian forces burned farms and public buildings in the countries they had occupied as they evacuated eastward. As Estonia is the northernmost Baltic state, Germany reached it last, first advancing from Poland and crossing through Lithuania and Latvia. It took the German army nearly a week to reach Estonia after the invasion of Poland began. In the meantime, the Red Army carried out a final campaign of terror as it retreated, burning farms and villages and, in some cases, executing thousands of Latvian, Lithuanian, and Estonian civilians.

Estonians like my parents viewed the German advance as a liberation. They often talked at length about the fate of our country and the prospects of returning. The hope in their voices would swell when talking about the strength of the German army. This belief in Nazi military might was buoyed by the conscription of many Estonian men into a battalion that was fighting on the advancing front. This included my father, who had been drafted into service. Fortunately he avoided combat because he developed an anemia which disqualified him. Uncle Fritz was placed into the reserves, but Paul was the family hero. He had been promoted to Major in the Estonian battalion and was leading the charge in re-taking our homeland.

A year of watching our Estonia languish under the iron fist of the Soviet forces had deepened the enmity between us and the Russians that began during the 1940 occupation. We viewed the German forces as heroes, Uncle Paul included, for casting out the Soviet oppressors. Though a return to independence was what we wanted, Nazi occupation at least brought a short period of relative peace.

By September of 1941 the battle lines between Germany and Russia had moved east past Tallinn, into Russian territory. My father and mother decided to return home and begin operating the family farm again, joined by Fritz. Paul was already there, recovering in a hospital in Tallinn from wounds he received during the liberation. I went with them, excited to see Uncle Paul and hear his war stories. But I was not prepared for the stark difference between the Estonia we had left and the desolation that we returned to. Our beautiful country had been laid waste, the land war-torn beyond all recognition. Nearly all public buildings had been destroyed. Many private homes and businesses had been burned and looted. Family friends had been killed or deported to labor camps in Siberia. In just one year, the government my grandfather had helped build was dismantled. My father's business was gone. Miraculously, the farm buildings at Uuemõisa had not been greatly harmed, but no other part of our lives was left untouched. The destruction of my home deeply impacted me, and to this day I can barely recall this return trip or even the happier times that came before. The experience of deep loss left a hazy mirage of pain that is hard to peel back and look behind.

The uneasy peace brought about by the German occupation of Estonia lasted for nearly three years as the Soviet Union and German Reich fought on the Leningrad front in Russia. During this time, we worked to rebuild our country. Rubble was cleared away, and buildings were rebuilt. Tallinn began to recover through the hard work of the Estonian people. Eventually, however, the strength of the German army faltered. A Soviet push into Estonia began in January of 1944 with the start of the Leningrad–Novgorod offensive, and the Battle of Narva began in February. Narva was on the border of Russia and Estonia, around 300 km to the East of Uuemõisa. Because of the strategic importance of the Narva isthmus, the German forces chose it for their final stand.

On March 9, 1944 my mother and I were visiting Tallinn to check in on my Uncle Paul. He had been in and out of the hospital there for the three years since his wartime injuries, and he was staying a few days for regular testing. On these occasions, I liked to bring him some home baked pastries and news from the farm, so that he didn't feel too left out. While we were at the hospital, news of a Soviet air raid arrived. We knew the fighting was close, but this had never happened before. My mother and I escaped south to home, 40 km away, before the barrage began. By 6:30 pm the explosions had started, and we spent the night listening to them while staring at the red sky on the northern horizon. All I could think about was Uncle Paul, who had chosen to stay and keep the nurses and other hospital residents comfortable. It was the first, though not the last, sleepless night I spent listening to bombs explode. We watched the red glow of our city burning, like some kind of fiery sunset that didn't know when to end. Ostensibly, the aim of the bombing was to cripple the German resupply efforts at the Baltic Sea port, but many of the bombs dropped on the Estonian capital were incendiary, and it seemed clear to us that the intent was to burn the city to the ground. The next morning, we tried to drive back to the hospital to search for Paul but found our way blocked by collapsed buildings and intense fires. The flames burned for several days, because Soviet saboteurs had disabled much of the city's water supply in advance of the air raid to make firefighting efforts harder. Nearly 20 percent of Tallinn burned, and 1000 civilians died. Uncle Paul was found under the rubble of the collapsed hospital wing where he had taken refuge under a surgery table with a nurse. The two of them were unharmed - protected from the collapse by the table's strong metal frame.

Until that day, we had hoped for a German defense of the eastern front, after which Estonia could negotiate for independence. But now, my father yet again began planning to flee west as the German lines seemed more and more likely to fail. The fighting continued through the summer of 1944 until, on September 5th, Finland signed a ceasefire with the Soviets and ended its fight with the Red Army. Until that point, the Fins had been providing air and sea support to the German defense of Eastern Estonia, including a counter-raid during the night of the Tallinn bombing on March 9th. The Finnish Air Force had joined forces with German aircraft to shoot down 10 of the attacking Soviet planes. Finland's peace treaty with the USSR left Estonia exposed by sea to the north, and nearly defenseless by air. The Soviet Union launched a comprehensive and overwhelming offensive push into Estonia on September 14, 1944.

Despite the horrific odds, we held out hope that the German forces - tens of thousands of which were conscripted Estonians - would resist the invasion. Estonians are a proud and patriotic people, with a deep love for our homeland that bolsters our drive to fight in her defense. But it was not enough. Only a few days later, on September 17th, news came that the USSR had pushed past the German defenses at Narva and were advancing across Estonia while the German troops withdrew. The Red Army was back.

The sounds of artillery grew louder and louder each day. At this point, I was only 9, but I was able to help my parents make preparations to evacuate. Unlike our exodus in 1941, when there was time to gather the necessary documents and arrange travel for the entire family, the 1944 displacement was violent and hurried from the start. The Russians had already shown us what kind of occupiers they would be, and the indiscriminate bombing of Tallinn had confirmed for us that they intended to re-occupy Estonia with an equally brutal grip. There was no question of whether to flee. My mother and I boarded a train that took us southwest to Austria where my father had arranged for us to stay with a friend in the city of

Linz. I desperately wanted my father to come with us, but he refused. He wanted to stay and fight.

After my mother and I were safely on our way south, Heino sat with his two brothers and agonized over what to do. Our family's ties to the Estonia government meant there was little chance they would be able to live on the farm unmolested once the Red Army troops arrived. He knew the last Russian occupation had been bloody; there was no reason to believe this would be any different. Yet the idea of fleeing a second time from the same forces that had killed thousands of our fellow Estonians was a bitter pill to swallow. The three brothers stayed together at Uuemõisa, debating their options and putting off the inevitable decision. The next day, word came that Tallinn was under attack and they knew that escape would soon be impossible. Each had to make their choice.

In the end, my father fled. He knew that going west to Germany would just be running toward more conflict, so instead he joined thousands of other Estonians in what later became known as "The Great Escape". Almost every seaworthy boat was used to ferry people across the Baltic sea toward safe harbor in Sweden and Finland. Not every ship made it safely across: some were attacked by Russian combat vessels, while others perished in the treacherous waters. My father had waited too long to be able to sail from Tallinn, so he went south to Pärnu and convinced a friend of his, Captain Tuulig, to bring him along when his boat set sail north for Sweden.

Both of my uncles decided to stay and joined the Forest Brothers. Neither had families of their own, and they preferred to resist Soviet rule directly through the guerilla warfare that began under the first USSR occupation. All three brothers - Heino, Paul, and Fritz - believed the Allies would liberate Estonia from Soviet rule once Germany was defeated.

When they separated in September of 1944, the brothers were hopeful that they would be reunited by Spring. However, when the war ended the following summer, they learned their hopes had been ill-founded. Instead of liberating the Baltic States, the United States and United Kingdom signed over the entirety of Eastern Europe, including Estonia, to the Soviet administration as part of the Potsdam Agreement. Estonia was used as a bargaining tool and handed over to Communist rule despite the atrocities of the first occupation and the desires of its people. It was a shocking, unthinkable outcome.

I never saw my uncles again. Decades later, after the Iron Curtain fell, I learned that both had died at the hands of the Russians. Paul was killed in 1947 during a skirmish between the Forest Brothers and Soviet security forces. Shortly after, Fritz was lured out of hiding by Russian agents who promised him safety in exchange for help running our family factory. When he appeared, they offered him an execution instead.

My grandmother also stayed in Estonia. Too old and stubborn to flee a second time, she lived hidden near the family farm in Vasalemma. While Paul and Fritz were alive, they provided her with a regular supply of food as well as clothes and fuel for the winter months. After they were killed, she was supported by the kindness of neighbors until she died in 1955. She never knew whether her son and grandson, my father and I, had escaped to safety.

Tom, age 1, with his mother Leida.
Estonia, 1935

Tom's father, Heino, in an Estonian military uniform.
Estonia, early 1930s

Tom at a party, age 4. Prior to the first invasion of Estonia.
Estonia, 1938

Uuemõisa, the Saar family farm. Located in the outskirts of
Tallinn. Taken after the war and occupations.
Estonia, 1990s

CHAPTER 2

Austria and Sweden

My mother and I departed Estonia for Linz, Austria, where we settled in to await word from my father. We were worried, but life in Linz was comfortable - especially when compared to our time in Berlin. I attended 4th grade there in Austria and, even though I was only 10 years old, I was recruited into Hitler's Youth.

I was just old enough to join the paramilitary youth organization of the Nazi Party. I was far from embracing the ideology of the Nazis, as the idea of the prowess of the mighty Germany army had lost its luster when we witnessed its failure to defend our homeland. We were in Austria as a direct result of this. Still, the organization was a boys group that taught outdoors skills and took trips into the mountains to hike and ski, and I enjoyed the camaraderie of the other boys. My mother reasoned that at my young age, there was no chance I would be directly recruited into the Nazi defense forces like some of the older boys. Fortunately, she was right.

I went on a few trips, despite frequent bombings in the area by Allied aircraft. On one occasion I remember distinctly, I was hiking up the side of a mountain with a group of other Hilter's Youth and we watched as an Allied bomber was intercepted by anti-air fire from the ground. We saw the plane start to smoke as the bullets hit it, then watched as it lost altitude, gradually at first, before plummeting toward the ground and crashing to its fiery end.

As the Soviet Union slowly advanced across Eastern Europe, we waited. After 3 long months, we still did not know whether my father had escaped. My mother and I began to come to terms with the possibility that he would not meet us in Austria. It was possible that he had decided to stay and fight. Worse, he may have been caught while trying to leave Estonia. It is difficult to find that balance between hope and resignation, but we had each other to lean on, and we did our best. Finally, after another 2 months had passed - almost half a year after fleeing Estonia, we received word from my father: he had found safe haven in Stockholm, Sweden. We dropped everything and prepared to leave Austria and join him.

During that time, the Spring of 1945, a trip from Austria to Sweden was a perilous one. The route ran north to Berlin, where we would have to change trains to head to the northern German coast. We would then board a ferry to cross the Baltic Sea. While Germany still controlled Berlin, the Soviet Union now controlled Poland, only about 60 miles to the east. Berlin was not far behind the line of battle, and Russia was frequently pressing into Germany toward Berlin. The front line was moving daily as German forces retreated. Unfortunately, the only alternative that we had was far too tenuous: wait until Germany fell, and then attempt to cross the border while in a newly Russian-occupied country. Given those two options, we left as soon as we could.

It was early March when we set out, boarding a train from Vienna to Berlin. As we rode through the rolling green countryside, Allied bombers flew overhead on their way to targets further into Germany. Explosions from the war I was leaving behind occasionally punctuated the night and created a terrifying staccato over the hum and grind of the north-bound train. It took us 6 hours, but finally, we arrived safely in Berlin.

I remember the deathly quiet that seemed to hang over the German capital. Berlin had not escaped the ravages of war: many of the buildings in this fiercely proud city had been reduced to rubble. I thought of how it compared to my own Tallinn, two cities torn apart by bombings, but I knew there was one important difference: Estonia did not want this war.

24

Germany, however, was being called to account for its hubris. As we waited in the central station for the train that would take us toward the coastal town of Grossenbrode, it seemed like the city had released a deep sigh, resigning itself to surrender.

Our train arrived, and we boarded and traveled to Grossenbrode without incident. There, we were able to board a ferry destined for Gedser, Denmark. Upon our arrival in the Danish city, we hit our first blockade: we were detained in the harbor alongside other arrivals by anti-German Danish partisans. They had occupied the docks and refused to let any of the ferry passengers pass into the country without proof of an "acceptable" destination or a personal connection. We waited for several tense hours while little headway was made. Finally, my mother managed to corner a taxi cab that had dropped off another passenger. She often used her good looks to convince men to help her, and this proved no exception. A warm smile and a few gestures was all it took to recruit the driver to provide us a clandestine ride out of the harbor. He even agreed to take us all the way north to Copenhagen, about two hours away. I ducked into the back seat, keeping low as we passed by the line of angry partisans. It was my first taste of infiltration.

Copenhagen is a mere 25 miles away from Sweden: tantalizingly close, but crossing the Öresund strait in between proved challenging. Denmark was still held by Germany while Sweden had remained neutral. Because of this, border crossings were highly scrutinized. We also had very little money left. My mother, enterprising as ever, found a shop willing to purchase the jewelry she had managed to bring along. She sold every piece. The proceeds of the sale, together with the little we had left, were enough to pay for the passage for us both.

Though the crossings from Copenhagen were heavily restricted, it helped that it was just my mother, a single woman, and me, a young boy. It still took several days to find a ferry that would take us, given our German documents. In the end, we had to travel north to Helsingor, Denmark and make the crossing there, finally arriving in Helsingborg, Sweden. Only a small straight separated the two towns - just 2.5 miles across - but I remember the crossing felt like passing into heaven. All the German-held territory we had passed through - Austria, Denmark, and Germany itself - had been suffering from electricity outages for years as the Allied bombers repeatedly crippled the power infrastructure. Helsingborg, with its cityscape lit up at night, was a beacon of safety and warmth I had almost forgotten was possible.

The next day, March 21, as if the war itself was hounding our travels northward, Copenhagen was bombed by the British Royal Air Force. It was the one and only time Copenhagen was the target of an air raid during WWII. The target, the Gestapo headquarters in the city, was destroyed, but 145 civilians were killed as well. It reminded me of our experience with the Russian bombing of Tallinn, and I try not to think very much about this second close call we had.

Together with my mother, I had escaped the advancing Soviet Union in Estonia by fleeing to Austria, from which we passed north along the war front to arrive safely in Sweden. Despite all the dangers we had faced along the way, we hadn't anticipated the personal conflict we were now faced with: my father's girlfriend. When we arrived in Stockholm on March 22, we were shocked to find that my father had taken in with another woman. She was also an Estonian refugee, and was pregnant with his child. My family, instead of being reunited, broke apart.

My mother divorced Heino and took me with her. We settled into a refugee home provided by the Swedish government. Similar to our experience in Germany, it was the private residence of a wealthy family. Set outside the city near the coast and nestled in rolling green hills, the property extended so far that I couldn't even see neighboring houses. It was a several mile walk to the nearest town community, but we were able to pass our time in the outdoor swimming pool built into the ground behind the large house. The fact that it was luxurious, especially considering our circumstances, didn't matter to me. I had been desperately waiting for the reunion with my father - I had imagined it a hundred times. But now he was gone; not taken by the Russians, not dead as we had feared, but gone all the same. Without my father I felt lost, and nowhere could feel like home to me. My mother, though heartbroken, found the strength to keep going and to provide for me. She took a job at the post office, where she worked hard to make enough money to keep us fed and clothed. Our living quarters within the refugee housing were well-furnished, but we didn't have much in the way of money. I recall many soups of simply boiled bones that she had purchased at restaurants or butchers shops. Things like coffee and meat were too expensive, and we couldn't afford them. Transportation and other luxuries were impossible. I, a 10-year-old boy who spoke Estonian and German but no Swedish, had to learn to live in this new kind of exile.

Sweden registered us and other Estonian refugees by issuing "Foreigner Passports". As if to emphasize our loss, our citizenship was noted as "Stateless". To add insult to injury, we were offered Russian citizenship, which we vehemently declined. So, instead, my documents reflected our new reality: Estonia, the country I was born in and had spent half my young life in, no longer existed in the diplomatic status quo.

WWII raged on outside of the safety we had found in Sweden, and there were constant reminders of it. We lived in a western suburb of Stockholm close to an area where the Swedish government was housing a group of US airmen. These pilots had been shot down over Germany and managed to escape to Sweden. Since they were safe in a neutral country, with no way to get home and no orders to return, they spent their time leisurely. They would stroll around town, sun themselves in the parks, and frequent the corner pubs after their monthly stop by the U.S. Embassy to collect wartime salary. They knew their combat service was over, and their cavalier nature was the cause of more than one Swede joking that perhaps they had shot each other down on purpose to come vacation in Scandinavia.

The war ended later that year in November of 1945. Our airmen neighbors finally left us, boarding ships destined for home in America. But no return home was possible for us. The war was resolved, but the Soviet Union retained an iron grip on Estonia and the rest of Eastern Europe. The Estonian state was effectively dissolved, and the continued occupation by Russia was now written into international law. There was no ambassador or head of state left to argue otherwise at the bargaining table, though some Americans overseeing the denazification of Germany advocated for pushing back against the influence of communism in Europe. One such leader was General George Patton. Unfortunately for Estonia and its neighbors, Patton died as the result of a car crash - purportedly accidental - and the Baltic states were swallowed up into the USSR.

This made it impossible for my parents and I to return safely, even if Russian propaganda began pouring into Sweden insisting otherwise. So long as the Soviet occupation continued, the political connections of the Saar family meant we would never be able to return. I was now 11 years old, and I turned to the task of learning the Swedish language and way of life. Fortunately, I was not alone. There were more than 200,000 refugees in Sweden in 1945, many of whom were Estonian or from other Baltic states. The Swedish effort to absorb displaced people from across Europe was largely successful, and the Estonian community founded churches, started schools, and built new lives. I attended one such Estonian school for grades 5 and 6. I then moved on to join a Swedish university preparatory school, called a gymnasium, where in addition to Swedish, I began to learn English and French. I graduated from gymnasium at 17 years old and took up a job as a clerk at a company importing goods from mainland Europe. It wasn't the career in international business that my parents had imagined for me when they hired Tata to teach me German, but it was something similar. I chose to continue studying during this time, attending night school at the College of Stockholm. I didn't know it at the time, but one day my fluency in 5 languages - French, German, Estonian, English and Swedish - would make me the perfect international liaison.

Eventually, my parents reconciled and realized a post-war family reunion. I got to know the step-sister my father now had and even babysat her on occasion as I was 10 years older than her. We lived out the following decade in relative peace.

Tom (front left) and his mother (middle) pose outside with their Austrian hosts.

Tom (Second from left) watches the wine pour around the dinner table.
Austria, 1944

Class photograph of Tom's secondary school in Stockholm, Sweden. Tom stands in the back row, fifth from the right. Sweden, 1945

CHAPTER 3

The Lodge Act

In 1952, the passage of a law half the world away changed my life forever. Across the Atlantic, United States Senator Henry Cabot Lodge, Jr. sponsored a bill that called for 2,500 single men from Eastern Europe to enlist in the United States Army. The law, which became known as the Lodge-Philbin Act or the Lodge Act, guaranteed U.S. citizenship to non-resident aliens who served at least 5 years and were honorably discharged. The goal was to recruit displaced men from the Eastern European countries and use their resentment toward the Soviet Union and cultural knowledge to spread anti-communist sentiment throughout Europe. In other words: the goal was to recruit men like me.

By 1952 the Cold War was in full swing. The Soviet Union had solidified its post-war supervisory role in Eastern Europe into full-blown occupation. After my own personal experience with the Russians during WWII, the thought of Estonia being permanently held by Russia was both devastating and infuriating. But I was a refugee, along with so many of my fellow Estonians, tucked up in a foreign country and doing our best to eke out a new life; there was nothing we could do. The political boundaries enforced by the USSR to keep occupied countries insulated from western influence, known as the Iron Curtain, were firmly in place. Contact with home was impossible. We were completely cut off from our home country and those who still lived there. Not everyone had been able to flee, and some had chosen to stay. I personally had escaped the clutches of communism, along with many others, but our flight from the Soviet takeover had fractured my family. Russia had stolen so many things from me that I could never get back: my happy childhood, my family farm, and my uncles and grandmother. The USSR was a brutal and sadistic regime, one that had proven that it cared nothing for its people or the people of the lands they stole. It had bombed our city and burned our towns, telling us in no uncertain terms that if they couldn't own our land, then they would make sure there was nothing left for anyone else to own. Over time, the pain of loss had changed from hurt to resentment, before finally hardening into hatred. So when, in 1953, news of the Lodge Act spread through the Estonian community in Sweden, I was determined to enlist. I knew America was directly involved in the peacekeeping in Europe and that anti-communism sentiment was a cornerstone of U.S. foreign policy. Enlisting in the U.S. Army would be a way to fight back, for the first time, against the evil empire who had driven me out of my childhood home.

My eagerness was shared by several close Estonian friends. There were no U.S. Army bases in Sweden, so together we devised a plan to ferry across the Baltic Sea to Germany to make our applications. The very first step was also the most difficult one: breaking the news to my mother. She loved me more than anything in the whole world, and after everything we had survived together, she was deeply protective. I broached the topic one night over dinner. "So Mom," I started cautiously, "have you heard the news out of America?"

"No, what's that, then?" She took another bite of the pork chops and sauerkraut that she had prepared. News from America was common.

"There's a call out for recruits. Non-American recruits. Promise of good pay and citizenship after 5 years. I'd just have to go to Germany and…. " I tailed off.

Her eyes had locked on to me with a withering intensity the moment I had said "recruits". I have no doubt she understood my desire to fight back, but it was clear that she thought no good could come from it. Going to the United

States however… It was the country leading the new world order. It was also very far away from the Russians. It was a good opportunity. Even she could see that. "Well..." She said calmly, after a few moments, "it sounds like you should go, then."

My jaw dropped. I had been preparing counter-arguments all afternoon. I had thought long and hard about the various points she might bring up, different things she might say, and what I could say in return to convince her this was the right choice. And after all that, I needed none of it. I was shocked, but relieved. The hardest part was over, and it hadn't even been as hard as I thought. As soon as I could manage, I quit my job as a clerk and made my travel plans. Details on the Lodge Act were scarce, but I was confident that if someone like myself, an eager recruit who perfectly fit the description of what they were looking for, presented himself at a U.S. Army Base, they'd take me in right away. So, together with my two close friends, we hitchhiked south to Malmo and ferried across to Germany.

I had assumed that the existence of the Lodge Act meant the U.S. Army would be excited to have men apply. But, unbeknownst to us in Sweden, the Lodge Act was largely a political move by Senator Lodge. In reality, it was unwelcome by the Army leadership who saw it not as a way to obtain much needed help, but rather as an organizational nightmare. When I arrived with my friends at the base in Seckenheim, Germany, there were dozens of other men seeking to apply as well. I filled out the forms with my personal details and sat down to wait. For hours, the Sergeants tasked with handling new arrivals reviewed application after application. Eventually, our paperwork was reviewed, accepted, and we were scheduled to take entrance exams the next week. This surprised me. I had thought that the U.S. Army was eager for help, but it became clear to me - both from the slow bureaucracy of the application and the presence of qualifying exams - that this was not quite the case.

Thousands of men applied for military service under the Lodge Act, but the U.S. Army had limited capacity to train European men who were deeply different from the standard American conscript. While fluent English was not officially required, the Army instituted a battery of exams to severely limit the number of people who were ultimately allowed to enlist.

We hadn't counted on the extra week in Seckenheim and the three of us had no money for a place to stay. We stretched what we had brought with us and did a few odd jobs around town to feed ourselves for a day at a time. When the exams arrived, my Swedish education shone through. Topics such as mathematics and English literacy were simple affairs for me, though I did notice those around me muttering in consternation during the session. Some of the exams felt more like IQ tests than knowledge checks, and I certainly wasn't prepared for the lie detector test asking after my family and potential communist connections.

Two Sergeants sat me down in a dull room with a single table that held the polygraph machine. After connecting me to a series of wires, one of the officers began gruffly asking me questions. Where was I born? During the occupation of Estonia, had my family ever received assistance from the Russian government? Did I have personal friends in the Red Army? While the test itself had surprised me, none of the questions unnerved me. I answered calmly and confidently - I had only hatred for the USSR and its communist regime.

At last, after three full days of testing, I was finished. I had been hopeful that a decision would be made promptly, but instead I was told it would take at least 6 months for the enlistment paperwork to be reviewed and approved. I was deflated, but there was nothing I could do. I accepted the ticket the Army provided for my trip home to wait for news. "We will send notice to your address," we were promised.

My experience was not unique. Many applicants waited months or even years to learn if their Lodge Act application was approved. The U.S. Army Counter-Intelligence Corps (CIC) was the source of the wait; the CIC performed background checks on each of the thousands of applicants. The Lodge Act recruitment occurred in the midst of the Red Scare of the early 1950s, and any familial or professional connection to the Communist party was grounds for disqualification. Often those who failed the background check never heard back from the U.S. Army at all, and were left to wonder if their paperwork was lost or if some other reason had prompted the rejection.

I didn't know any of this at the time, and after 6 months waiting impatiently in Sweden, I decided to return and press the issue. I traveled back to the base in Seckenheim where I had submitted my original application. I had already quit my job, anticipating the call to enlist to arrive at any point so I had nothing to lose taking the trip. Though I had the support of my parents, I did not have much money for the second journey. Undeterred, I planned the familiar route: hitchhike from Stockholm to Malmo and ferry across to Germany. From there, I would need to either hitchhike again or try to find work to pay for the rest of the train fare.

It was June of 1954 when I made my solo trip back to Seckenheim. I settled on hitchhiking to conserve money, and upon arriving, I immediately inquired after my application. Recruitment officers informed me it was still pending, and there was no way to expedite the process. I was frustrated. I had quit my job so that I would be able to join the U.S. Army at the drop of the hat, and here they were, dragging the process out for months. I had no money left for the return journey, and even if I had, I was concerned that if I went back to Sweden, I might never hear back at all. So, unwilling to give up on what might be my only chance to join the fight against Russia, I decided to find a way to stay in Germany.

A few hungry days of wandering led me to an Estonian labor force. It was a collection of men who had served as infantry in the Nazi army after the Waffen-SS had conscripted an Estonian battalion to defend against the Russian advance. Though none of them recognized my Uncle Paul's name, several had served during the 1941 liberation of Estonia. Now that the war was over, they were unwelcome in Russian-occupied Estonia due to their military service for Germany and had banded together to live and work in Germany under the new American occupiers. Nearly 200 strong, the group had a regular kitchen, cook, and mess hall. I was able to secure a dry place to sleep and a warm meal to eat in exchange for serving as kitchen help. The work was both grueling and boring. I grew to hate the drudgery of peeling potatoes for hours each morning only to spend hours more washing the dishes at night. Still, I was grateful to have somewhere to stay as I waited for my application to clear. I was living with Estonias who had fought against Russia, and I hoped that I would soon be an American soldier continuing the same fight.

To be honest, it wasn't all boredom. I found that if I was fast enough with the dishes, then the evenings were mostly free. I made friends quickly, and some weekend nights I would join a few other fellows and hitch a ride to nearby towns to visit new pubs. One night while out drinking, I remember seeing an extra-large group of women surrounding one fellow at the bar. Nudging a nearby friend, I pointed and asked, somewhat enviously, "Who's that bloke?"

"That's Elvis," my friend replied in surprise, "You've heard of Elvis, right?" The incredulous look on his face made it clear that he was shocked I hadn't recognized him myself. I hadn't ever heard of Elvis Presely before then, but I got to meet him that night in Germany. Only later did I come to realize how significant that coincidental meeting really was.

CHAPTER 4

The United States

In November 1954, nearly a year after my initial application and 5 months after I began peeling potatoes for the Estonian labor force, I finally received word from the U.S. Army that I was to report for enlistment. I was ecstatic. I immediately wrote to my mother to share the good news. The exciting new future I had been chasing for more than a year was about to begin.

The persistence I demonstrated by arriving and staying until an approval was delivered is one of the reasons I was one of just 1,302 successful Lodge Act enlistees. Thousands upon thousands of men applied and were turned away, but my unique combination of interest, education, and Estonian background made me an ideal choice. Though I didn't know it at the time, I was also one of the last enlistees. The Lodge Act recruitment program ran from June 25th 1950 to July 29th 1954. I applied in early 1954 and was sworn into service of the U.S. Army on Dec 17th, 1954 alongside 2 other Estonians and a mix of 8 others: Lithuanians, Poles, and Czechs.

I had several weeks before I was to leave, so I spent New Years Eve 1954 in Zweibrücken, Germany. As one of the fresh recruits, I was invited to a celebration with other American soldiers. It was my first experience of social life in the U.S. Army, and it was a lively one. A four-piece band played music and I joined the other soldiers - new and old - regaling each other with tales of home. Everyone was friendly, the drinks flowed freely, and as I watched the clock tick from 1954 to 1955, it truly did feel like a new beginning.

After months of subsisting in the Estonian labor force, enlistment felt like luxury. I was granted a new uniform and a bunk of my own in the unit's barracks. A few days after New Years I began the journey to the United States via train to Bremerhaven. There, along with the other Lodge Act recruits, I boarded an Army troop transport ship bound for basic training in the United States. The trans-Atlantic journey took six full days. It was during this trip that I discovered how lucky I was to not be afflicted by seasickness - many of my fellow passengers were sick the whole time, and some for several days after. Fortunately, I was spared. Still, for one reason or another, everyone was eager to land at Fort Dix in New Jersey. I could not wait to begin basic training. It was time to get to work.

My basic training was my first experience of the United States. The eight-week program was easy. While others found it challenging, I had no difficulty with the physical conditioning, and the emotional conditioning was mild compared to my childhood experiences with war. Basic training was the first step in achieving the goals that had motivated me to enlist, and though I had never been in combat, much of my childhood had been touched by WWII. I wanted revenge for the pain the Russians had inflicted on my family and my homeland, and this was the first time in my life I felt I was moving closer to achieving that goal. So, when officers from the 10th Special Forces Group passed through Fort Dix to talk to the Lodge Act recruits, I was a keen listener.

The Sergeant snapped off a list of reasons to join his unit. "You make more money, you do cooler shit, and you don't have to listen to some engineer tell you how to dig a ditch. What's not to like?" His description of the work was equally succinct, saying, "$50 per jump, and you jump a lot at jump school. It's called jump school for a reason."

I listened thoughtfully. I didn't love the idea of jumping out of planes with nothing but a nylon parachute strapped to my back, but for $50 at a time… I returned to listening to the Sergeant.

"The 10th executes the most important and dangerous missions of any Army unit. You'll go behind enemy lines. You'll kill from the shadows, you'll help bring down the Soviets from within and leave no trace. It ain't easy, but…"

Now *this* had my mind racing. Dark memories of desperate flights from advancing Russians danced through my mind, mixing in with dreams of daring new adventures. It was a potent combination. Now that he wasn't talking about planes anymore, I found the Sergeant's pitch more compelling. This sounded like the best chance I would have to help free Estonia just like my Uncle Paul had.

"How do we sign up?" I blurted out. The group of recruits who had been sitting around listening to the pitch turned and looked at me. The Sergeant smiled broadly.

"Right this way, son".

I was assigned to go from basic training to airborne training for the Special Forces 10th at Fort Bragg in North Carolina. It would be about a month until I shipped south, so it was the perfect opportunity to take leave and explore New York City, which was just 75 miles north of Fort Dix. I was keen to feel the hum of the biggest city the country had to offer, and truly experience the America I had heard so much about while in Europe. Along with several other soldiers who would be joining me to train at Fort Bragg, I took 14 days leave and rode a train into Manhattan. We found lodging at a YMCA and filled our days by wandering the city and seeing the Statue of Liberty and other iconic sights. We also went to watch several baseball games at Yankee Stadium. Baseball was uniquely American and it was exhilarating to sit in a crowd of thousands of cheering and jeering New Yorkers and watch the strange game play out over its three hour duration. It was plenty of time to drink a few beers and learn both the rules of baseball and how to be an American.

Soon enough it was time to return to duty and board the train to Fort Bragg. Fortunately there was a bar on the train, and many of us bought drinks to help ease ourselves through the transition back into service. It worked, right up until the train crossed into North Carolina. North Carolina was a "dry" state at the time, so as soon as we crossed the state border, the train had to stop selling alcohol. I was not the only new recruit who was disappointed by this, but it was probably for the best that we arrived at Fort Bragg to begin our training mostly sober.

Transferring to the 10th SFG meant attending jump school, just like the Sergeant had promised. Some of the missions would require air drops behind enemy lines, so all members had to be jump certified. If you failed out of jump school, you were doomed to reassignment to a more menial duty. I wasn't going to let that happen to me.

Jump school, however, was significantly more strenuous than basic training. Everything was taken to the extreme. Walking was banned: all recruits had to "double-time" wherever we went, jogging to and from our destinations. There was a metal bar set up across the doorway at the entrance to the mess hall where anyone entering or exiting had to make 10 pull-ups. The physical routine was so strenuous the water available to drink was mixed with salt to compensate for what was lost by sweating. This was far harder than basic training and I reveled in the challenge and in competing with my fellow soldiers to maintain composure despite the intensity of the daily routine. For me, jumping was the most stressful part of it all.

I was 3,000 meters in the air and staring out the open side of a C-47 airplane when I found my resolve truly tested for the first time. Amidst the roar of the plane engines and the terribly loud wind, a strange moment of quiet arrived when it was time to take my first jump. "Jumping" was a bit of an exaggeration, as you mostly shuffled sideways and fell. I had been instructed on how to fall so as to avoid spinning out of control, how to deploy my parachute, and when to do it. But none of that was on my mind in the final moment before a jump. It was as if my entire life had rushed right up to that second and paused. In that pause, I forgot everything and stared out the back of the plane. My mind blanked. It was as if the War had never happened, as if I had never fled home, as if I was just about to fall out of a plane by accident.

The man in front of me started shuffling over and fell out the open door. Suddenly it was my turn. Robotically, I turned and fell. Time rushed back to full speed. Suddenly unfrozen, my mind ran briskly through my training as I traced the square cornfields below looking for the landing destination. Slowly the lines grew bigger, but slower than I had expected. After 30 seconds, the other recruits who had jumped before me started deploying their chutes. I watched them pop open below me, one after the other as I followed their trajectory downwards. After the designated time, I deployed my own parachute and lurched into a slow final descent.

As I drifted down, a scream came hurtling by me to the right. Whipping my head around, I caught a glimpse of a soldier falling past me without their 'chute deployed. He should have opened it by now - there must be some problem keeping his parachute from opening correctly. My eyes followed them downward, realizing the fellow had less than 10 seconds to figure it out. Impossibly, the plummeting soldier landed on top of the parachute of another soldier. He grappled with the nylon, trying to find purchase. And he did! The two men veered off course in a spiral descent. They took a hard landing that left a few bruises but, thankfully, there were no dead soldiers that day.

Besides jumping out of planes, I was taught a wide range of skills that I would need in order to accomplish the 10th SFG's mission of "Unconventional Warfare". This included demolition, intelligence tradecraft, escape and evasion, use of explosives and weapons of all kinds, and hand-to-hand combat. There was even a special session on how to break the necks of unsuspecting enemy combatants.

The training wasn't merely theoretical instruction. The Allied commanders knew that the Soviet army far exceeded the

Allied forces present in Europe, and that they would not be able to hold the front line that had been drawn across Germany if the Russians launched an offensive like the one used to overwhelm Nazi Germany. Instead, Allied leadership planned to delay, disrupt, and distract any advancing Soviet force long enough to establish more favorable battle lines further West. This strategy led to the idea of a covert force capable of embedding behind an advancing Russian army and engaging in a shadow war. But such a unit didn't exist in the U.S. Army; thus, in 1952, the 10th Special Forces Group, called the 10th SFG or the 10th Group, was created in 1952 to fulfill this specific need. The Special Forces were authorized to undertake extreme tests to ensure their men were prepared for anything. It was common for the unit commanders to fly soldiers to inhospitable destinations and have them jump out with minimal supplies and the vague goal of "getting back home". A few weeks into my time at Fort Bragg, I was dumped unceremoniously into the Florida Everglades with a 0.45 pistol and only one magazine. This was the espionage equivalent of a practice jump, and we would end up doing many such live exercises. I found my way out over several days without injury, if you don't count hundreds of mosquito bites.

The ultimate goal of our training was to prepare for a wartime crisis in Europe by creating a group of soldiers who could work undercover and behind enemy lines to spy and sabotage. The novelty of our mission meant our training was equally unique. While jump school and hand-to-hand combat were common to other elite units in the Army, the 10th SFG also practiced more exotic maneuvers. I gained experience in exiting an underwater submarine to achieve a covert beach landing, as well as nighttime parachute drops with only ground flares to help judge the distance to the ground and how level the drop zone was.

I was one of just 100 Eastern European volunteers who joined the special forces through the Lodge Act. Some intended to join but failed out of jump school or at other points in the training regimen. Many others resisted recruitment to the special forces and preferred assignment to more routine duties. But for me, the tragic degradation of my family and home at the hands of the Russian military gave me the intensely focused motivation required to excel in this training. I would never have joined the U.S. Army, not to mention the Special Forces, if it weren't for my own experience of Russian-enforced exile. The Lodge Act may have enabled my recruitment, but Russia itself had motivated it. I saw it as a way to retaliate by playing a part in the destruction of the regime that had forced my family into exile. I had already devoted myself to the cause, and I was finally ready for action.

CHAPTER 5

North Korea

Frustratingly, as these things often go, my first deployment wasn't against Russia.

The Korean War ended with the signing of the Korean Armistice Agreement in 1953, but the United States was still actively supporting South Korea as I was finishing training at Fort Bragg. None of the rank-and-file members of the 10th SFG knew, but American support in Korea sometimes took the form of special forces operations behind enemy lines. It was advantageous to capture North Korean soldiers for interrogation and use in prisoner swaps, so special forces units would deploy into territory held by the North with the goal of gathering intelligence and capturing hostages.

I was assigned to do exactly that for my first mission. The plan was straightforward: jump into hostile territory under cover of darkness, identify a vulnerable patrol route, capture its soldiers, and extricate the hostages undetected to South Korea. I was nervous, but I preferred to think about the operation as just another training exercise; we had undertaken dozens over the last year in the United States. Unfortunately, there was plenty of time on the long flight over the Pacific to ponder the differences. The one that struck me the most was that training always had emergency aid on standby. On foreign soil, however, American forces could not directly support or even acknowledge our actions. Not only was failure permanent, but even success would be swept under the rug as if it had never happened. The goal was to be ghosts - the kind that took hostages.

It was important that there was no evidence Americans had been in North Korea. Our capture, or the discovery we had been there at all, could cause political tension and weaken the armistice agreement. Every precaution was taken, including three days of eating a strictly Korean diet prior to the operation so that any toilet pits we left in the woods would appear to have come from locals.

Because there were no pre-installed friendly forces on the ground, a drop zone could not be arranged. Instead, my five teammates and I were to jump under the cover of darkness with the aim of landing in a lake about 25 miles north of the North/South Korean border. We had one last hot Korean meal, suited up, and boarded the C-47 which would drop us. The jump went without incident and we splashed down undetected. The lake water was cold - it was October, after all - but we dragged our soggy rucksacks to shore and slowly made our way through the woods along a predetermined course that would place us near a North Korean outpost.

Over the next several days, the six of us watched every movement in and out of the enemy encampment. The goal was to choose between the trickle of supply shipments and patrol trucks that came and went and pick one to intercept. The ideal target would be manned by one or just a few men, and follow a consistent schedule and route. One patrol that left early every morning met every target criteria. Each day at exactly 0630 hours a truck manned by two men rolled out of the base to tour the nearby woods. It was otherwise unarmed and we could easily overpower the drivers as long as we had the element of surprise. After watching for one more day - just to be sure - we executed our plan.

The night before the strike we positioned ourselves close to the road, moving cautiously and covering our tracks as we went. An hour before the light, we quietly assembled a roughshod blockade of large limbs and a few rocks we could move into place quickly and hid nearby. We were too far from the base to see if the gates had opened as expected, so I was relieved to hear the rumbling of the truck engine as it came down the forest road, right on time. It crept closer, coming into sight and then to an abrupt halt as the driver spotted the impasse. In unison, we leapt from hiding and brandished our pistols, yelling in English at the driver and his companion. The North Koreans reacted too slowly to defend themselves, and after a few chaotic moments of shouting, we had them out of the truck and gagged. We cut the truck's cables to make it harder to recover, and walked quickly into the forest with our two captives at gunpoint. It was all over in less than 10 minutes. Not a shot had been fired.

We returned with our hostages to the reconnaissance camp and prepared to extract back to South Korea. Having two uncooperative hostages in tow meant it would take three or four days to traverse the 25 miles of forest between us and the border, whereas without captives we might have made the passage in one. The North Korean outpost would surely miss the patrol in a few hours, so the first day of the escape was the most important. We moved as quickly as care would allow, traveling far enough from the kidnapping site to avoid the initial searches. After that, we spent several days moving slowly, painstakingly covering our track as we passed southward. It was far more important to go unnoticed than to be quick. We crossed the border into South Korea without incident.

After a few days, it became clear the plan to learn about the North Korean defenses and then use the hostages as bargaining chips wasn't going to work: the two men we captured proved resistant to questioning. I left that business to the American civilians who the Army was working with - likely CIA, I was never sure and made a point to never ask - but I was about to get my first taste of the sudden ruthlessness that characterized covert operations. Neither of the operation's goals required *two* hostages.

The civilian agent, myself, and several other boys took the two North Koreans on a helicopter ride out over the forest.

Once we were safely clear of the city outskirts, they opened the side door and made it clear to our unfortunate captives that there were two options: talk or "fly". Still, neither Korean spoke a word. I watched as two Americans picked one of the North Koreans up by the collar and unceremoniously threw him out of the helicopter. The fellow plummeted into the night with a shriek. Wide-eyed, the remaining hostage stared after his colleague for a moment then began talking rapidly in Korean. I held onto my seat so tightly my knuckles turned white, working down a tumult of emotion as I stared into the night. The helicopter turned and headed back to the city center. The image of the North Korean slowly falling out of sight played over and over in my head as we rode.

CHAPTER 6

Germany

The Korean excursion provided me with a first taste of what it was like to operate in hostile territory. Though the 10-day ordeal had gone smoothly, I preferred the comfort of a bunk to the hard forest floor, and I was glad to return to the United States after the mission was complete. I had joined the U.S. Army to aid in its anti-communist agenda, but I wanted to fight Russia in Europe, not Asia - and the disposal of the uncooperative North Korean soldier had left a bad taste in my mouth. I wanted to end the Russian occupation of my home. I was a good soldier, but I'll admit that at that point, in the back of my mind, I couldn't help but wonder if I had made a mistake.

Fortunately, less than two months after returning to the United States, I received orders to deploy to Germany. My success in Korea had apparently been noticed, and I was told to join other recruits to reinforce the men of the 10th SFG who were already stationed in Europe. I was ecstatic, and my doubts evaporated. If Korea was anything to base my expectations on, I'd soon be deep in Russian territory; maybe even able to travel as far as Estonia. I had plenty of time on the journey East across the Atlantic to dream of a return home.

In 1955, the 10th SFG operated in the Allied-occupied half of Berlin, but its original German headquarters had been at Bad Tölz, a town nestled deep in the Bavarian Alps. The unit still occupied the site and used it for training and staging operations outside the encircled capital city. All new recruits arriving from training in the United States were stationed there first to adjust to operating as part of an active combat unit.

We made landfall in the German town of Bremerhaven after nearly 7 days at sea. I was grateful for the solid feeling of the docks under my feet, even if the back-breaking work of unloading the boat began immediately. While training at Fort Bragg had been intense, it still had not fully prepared me for the level of hypervigilance the unit in Germany maintained. Every soldier had to live as if the next war was about to begin. Whereas I had been surprised by the walking ban during my training in North Carolina, in Germany the level of intensity was even higher. All weapons, travel supplies, and vehicles had to be ready for war at all times. This was in addition to the normal operations of an Army base in the United States.

To make the constant vigilance feel worthwhile to us of the rank-and-file, the commander of the unit loved to spring escape and evasion exercises on us. That, at least, was the same as my time training in the United States. Just one day after we arrived in Germany, I was relaxing in the temporary quarters that had been established at a hotel in Bremerhaven when a Sergeant strolled in.

"Saar, I've just reported you as a deserter."

"What's that, sir?" I said, standing quickly. I already knew this was likely an escape and evasion exercise (an E&E as the commander liked to call them) but it was always worth checking before you scurried off into the woods and got counted as a *real* deserter.

"I reported that you defected to the Soviet Union upon arrival in Germany. German law enforcement believes you have stolen important information about Special Forces operations and have been waiting for your arrival in Europe to defect to our enemies." The Sergeant paused for dramatic effect.

"The Krauts - the local police - will be hunting you. Get out of here, get out of that uniform, and report to the barracks in Bad Tölz once you arrive." The officer turned to walk out.

My heart sank as I realized Bad Tölz was over 400 miles to the South. It would take weeks to travel on foot, and I wasn't going to have time to pack any supplies.

"Good luck, son". The benediction came over the Sergeant's shoulder as he closed the door. I sprung into action. If it was too far on foot, I would have to find another way. For now, I walked calmly out of the hotel, pretending I was headed out on a stroll to take in the evening air. Even though dusk was falling, no one seemed inclined to stop me. I didn't know whether that was because the alarm hadn't been sounded yet, or if the other soldiers had been instructed to let me go for now, but either way, I was grateful.

The hotel serving as our temporary quarters was on the eastern outskirts of town, close enough that I was walking between houses almost immediately. The cobblestone pedestrian streets wound toward the center of town, and once I was out of sight I slowed my pace and formulated a plan. My most immediate concern was shedding my uniform. The poorly cut khaki fatigues clearly marked me as a member of the U.S. Army, and I had no idea how long I had before the "evasion" part of the mission would begin in earnest. This wasn't a life or death exercise; if I was caught I would simply be brought back to base to debrief how to improve for the next time. But my pride and reputation were on the line. Word of my successful mission in Korea had gotten around the unit, and being hauled back just miles from the start would be embarrassing. Was that why I had been picked to be the runner for this E&E? Did they think I needed more training? I had hoped evasion exercises would be less common now that I was in Germany. Yet here I was. I pushed the questions from my mind and focused on the task at hand: how to lose a uniform.

At my casual pace it was another 10 minutes before I reached the town center. I had another destination in mind, however. The main street was lined with restaurants, pubs, and one jazz club. I sauntered up to the club doors, nodded smoothly at the fellow standing watch outside, and sidled in.

Blessedly, no one was donning or depositing a coat in the entryway as I arrived. That would have made this trickier. I quickly browsed the selection and found a fine black overcoat that would cover most of my attire - there was nothing to be done about the boots - and ducked back out into the evening. No one said a word as I strode away in my new overcoat.

That's where my plan ended, however. I had no money for a train fare, no car to drive, and the Weser river that connected south to Bremen was too large to navigate on anything but a passenger vessel. As I walked aimlessly, I was struck with a strong recollection of the last time I had been cast out of an Army base and left to wander a German town without much of a plan: after trying to enlist as a Lodge Act soldier. Suddenly, I knew what to do. There had been Estonians in Seckenheim that had taken me in while I waited for the Army to do its background checks. Surely here in Bremerhaven there would be Estonians too. But how to find them?

I walked to a less affluent part of town, eyeing the houses for any sign they might be home to someone from the north. Finding no hints, I picked one at random. Knocking on the door, I put on my most endearing smile and waited. It opened to reveal a middle aged gentleman, cleanly cut and wearing glasses. He was German. Damn. I spoke rapidly in Estonian, asking for help even though I knew this fellow would not understand me. After a second's confusion, the man replied, speaking slowly in German,

"Sorry, I cannot help."

The door slammed shut. I repeated my plea at several other doors in the neighborhood. I wasn't after charity, instead I hoped that eventually one of the town's residents would recognize the Baltic language and point me to someone who would help. However, after three attempts I began to feel conspicuous. A young man knocking on random doors speaking Estonian? It wasn't working and it was going to get me caught.

I passed a phone booth, and stepped in. Like many booths it contained a phone book. Slowly, I scanned through the pages, full of German names, looking for one that stood out as Estonian. Finding one, I noted down the address next to the name. I didn't know the town well, but managed to make my way there. I put on my smile one more time and knocked.

An old lady answered the door. I paused and considered what to do, then decided to tell her the truth. There was no reason to lie, and I didn't like lying if I could avoid it. I told her I was training with the U.S. Army to help fight the Russians and hoped to return to Estonia some day. I explained the training exercise and why I had to travel in disguise to avoid my fellow soldiers. Her wrinkled eyes alternatively widened in surprise and narrowed with suspicion at each new detail. It was hard to tell if she was sympathetic. But, there was nothing to be done except finish - and as I did, I explained I needed a place to hide tonight if she was willing to help.

There was a moment of weighty silence after I finished my unlikely explanation. But when she replied it was in a motherly tone,

"Yes of course," She paused for a moment. "You must come in."

She widened the door and moved back toward the kitchen to fix me a warm cup of tea. As she did, I continued to explain that I had to travel south to Bad Tölz, but I had no money to purchase the train fare with. If the request for money was a stretch to her hospitality, she didn't show it. She immediately agreed to provide the fare.

The next day I boarded a train south, passing through the countryside and arriving at Bad Tölz in the evening. I reported in immediately and shocked the post commander, who congratulated me for my success; the rest of the unit hadn't even arrived from Bremerhaven yet.

Though it was merely training, the tools I used to succeed in the escape and evasion exercise - leveraging my own language and culture in a foreign country- was precisely

53

why Lodge Act soldiers were so useful to the U.S. Army Special Forces. The Americans, Poles, Czechs, Estonians, Lithuanians and Latvians all had a common enemy in the Russians. But Eastern Europeans had something the United States did not: a vast network of displaced civilians who were deeply sympathetic to anti-Russian causes. In every city in Germany there was an Estonian woman like the one who helped me travel south incognito. While it was possible for American soldiers to learn Baltic languages like Estonian, and many did, looking and acting like a European was much easier when you were one.

Training exercises like my first German escape and evasion were infrequent, but they were common enough to supply the unit with a constant stream of stories to tell. They were also essential to the core mission of the 10th SFG, keeping the men focused on operational readiness rather than the existential threat of Soviet invasion. In one outlandish operation, three men were tasked with infiltrating the British Army Headquarters and leaving the commander a note while he slept. I wasn't one of the three men assigned to join, and wasn't sure what point the 10th SFG brass was trying to make. It didn't matter much: orders were orders. The men went in and out, leaving a "You are Dead" note on the bedroom table of the Royal Army General.

CHAPTER 7

Berlin

Since the 10th SFG was headquartered in Berlin, it was not long before we transferred there. Operating in West Berlin was vastly different from Bad Tölz or anywhere else in Germany I had been. When I arrived in 1955, Berlin was two cities, with the East under Russian control and the West under Allied supervision. The city itself was surrounded by Soviet territory and though it was defended by a detachment of Allied forces, it was an island of Allied influence in an ocean of Russian occupation. By agreement with Soviet military authorities, one train per day was permitted to pass through the occupied countryside to Frankfurt, and then return with reinforcements and supplies. Every soul and shipment on board was documented by both sides, and because the 10th SFG was a shadow unit, we traveled as if we were regular members of the Seventh Army, the group leading the defense of the American quadrant of Berlin. It was essential that the number of 10th SFG men operating within Berlin and the surrounding areas was kept secret.

The incognito nature of the 10th SFG extended beyond our travel in and out of Berlin. Though the unit's officers had established a headquarters, they encouraged us to find places to live elsewhere in the city so our coming and going would be more discreet. Some took the opportunity to become friendly with West Berlin women, many of whom were happy to oblige an American man with spending money. We rarely wore uniforms, and the Army supplied me with civilian clothes to go along with a carefully crafted cover story wherein I worked as a dishwasher for a local restaurant. The unit was so dispersed that I rarely saw the other men, and instead we formed informal operative groups. Only the commanding officer of the 10th truly knew where our unit's members were and what they were doing. This protected all of us, as capture of one of our own by the Russains could not lead to the exposure of the whole unit. We were even provided with cyanide capsules, carefully sewn into our undergarments. If our only alternative was informing on our fellow soldiers or torture at the hands of the Soviets, the capsule was our way out. Not even the officers of Berlin's defense forces knew how many Special Forces soldiers were operating in their theater.

One of the 10th SFG's standing orders was to learn the location of Russian nuclear storage facilities, so that, in case of an invasion, we could stay behind and cripple the enemy's nuclear capabilities. The coordinates and contents of the facilities were highly sensitive. It was simultaneously the most important and most difficult information for us to discover. Fortunately, the Soviet-occupied half of the city was full of anti-Russian sentiment. After becoming oriented with the city layout and fully establishing my cover, my first missions involved using my Swedish passport to travel into East Berlin and search out citizens who may be willing to help the Allies. Like I had throughout my training, I relied on my Estonian background to connect with potential guerillas. Estonians hated the Russians almost without exception and they were easily recruited to our cause once they knew I was Estonian as well. I quickly built a small network of anti-communist sympathizers, and it was simple to have them pass me news about Soviet troop and supply movements. Such information wasn't immediately actionable, but over time it would allow me to identify unique convoys that could contain nuclear arms or hint at construction of a new storage bunker. It was slow but rewarding work.

I spent most days acting out a civilian life while keenly observing those around me. The Russians were constantly sending agents to West Berlin much like the Americans were sending us into East Berlin, and any change in behavior by a citizen might be a clue to uncovering a Russian operative. Observations and movements of known or suspected enemy agents were passed to the other men of the 10th SFG for monitoring. Sometimes, these surveillance efforts paid life-saving dividends.

In the summer of 1956, one of the 10th SFG men became known to Russian intelligence. As far as I knew, the Russians had never suspected me directly. I had the advantage of speaking five languages, including English, and carrying a legitimate Swedish passport. In fact, even though I was an American soldier, I had only been to America a few months' time during basic training and jump school. I looked, sounded, and acted European, because I was. Why would the Russians suspect me of being an American soldier? But the soldier the Russians had sniffed out hadn't grown up in Europe. He was from New England, and it was likely he let the Latvian accent he used as cover slip while visiting East Berlin. This put not only the soldier himself but his direct contacts within the unit at risk, and command began arranging to have him extracted from Berlin permanently. It would cost us his undercover connections in East Berlin, but the only other option was to find a way to convince the Russians he had left before they removed him permanently themselves. Fortunately, Russia employed American-looking fellows to work as spies much the same way America used Europeans like me. There was a Russian agent that I had been surveilling for several months who had the same stature and general facial features as my compromised American friend. I hatched a plan.

It took a few days to track down the Russian agent. Once I did, I shadowed him for a few days more, noting he generally left the West for the East every other day with the morning work time rush. I then headed to East Berlin myself. The 10th SFG knew of several bars in the East where an errant whisper would make its way directly to Russian intelligence.

While I wasn't sure if it was the owner or the regular patrons, it was easy enough to feed rumors to these eager informants. I went, had a beer, and let it "slip" that the compromised American soldier would make a crossing into East Berlin at the same time that the Russian agent traveled there. Perhaps they would apprehend their own man without realizing it. The next day I watched the daily crossing of the Russian agent. The Russians had taken the bait, and arrested their own man. Several days later we learned through informants that the fellow, unable to convince his captors of the mix-up, had been taken to the outskirts of the city and summarily executed. Meanwhile, my American comrade was spared this fate and was free to continue building his undercover network behind enemy lines.

My life of surveillance in West Berlin was punctuated by these infiltrations of the East. The most common reason I had for crossing the heavily monitored border was to make contact with civilians within my own network, but I also would meet with fully embedded American soldiers to receive their reports. Building spy networks based solely on recruits from the local populace was slow, and therefore the 10th SFG also relied on soldiers deployed on long-term assignment to operate on the Russian side of the Iron Curtain. This allowed us to maintain a steady flow of information from the East to the West, using a variety of spycraft techniques to alert each other to threats or to call meetings. Leaving a specific mark on the corner of an agreed-upon building or a stone resting at the base of a lamppost would trigger a visit from a soldier from the West - a soldier like me. I would make the border crossing the next day and tour a set of potential meeting places until I found the agent who left the mark. Often I would not know them in advance - these were men who had been living in East Berlin longer than I had been in the 10th. Both parties relied upon cues like an armband color to know we had the right man.

On one such occasion an American agent in East Berlin left a mark requesting an urgent evening meeting. I was to make the rendezvous at night inside a local restaurant. Crossing back over to West Berlin at night was a recipe for trouble, so I planned to stay the night at one of the safe houses set up across the Eastern half of the city. It wasn't something I liked to do; I always slept fitfully in the dimly lit townhouse basements the 10th had set up for these operations. The plan was to cross over mid-afternoon, make a show of visiting a relative in a residential district near the restaurant, and then attend the informant meeting.

Everything went smoothly until I got to the restaurant. There was a young couple milling about outside the main entrance and even though there was a light drizzle coming down, the fellow was holding his hat in his hand, too preoccupied gesturing and talking to his partner to notice the moisture slicking back his hair. A couple's row, perhaps, and I slid by them and approached the door. There was a small entryway, 2 meters long, preceding a second door into the restaurant. This sort of thing was common enough and kept the cold air of the street from ruining the warmth inside each time a new patron entered. Shaking the rain off my overcoat, I approached the inner door and peered through a small head-height window set into the wood.

It was better to plan a covert meeting at night when the restaurant was full, but even though it was dinner-time, the room I could see through the entryway window was nearly empty. Where there should have been two dozen people enjoying a meal, there were less than ten. But the real problem was that every person in the room was looking at one man, who was sitting at a table in the back left. Three men were standing around him, their backs to the door. I could just make out the sitting man's face and recognized him as the man I was there to meet. He was gesturing with his hands, the silver from the utensils reflecting the light as he did. And I saw the problem: my contact had switched his fork back into the right hand after cutting the meat on his plate. No German or Russian would eat like that; it was the American way. And an American

59

pretending to be a German in East Berlin in 1956 could only mean one thing: you were a spy.

The meeting's cover was blown. Protocol was to leave and reestablish contact at a later point, but this fellow was in serious trouble. Thinking quickly, I tried to figure out whether I could provide a distraction to give him a chance to make a run for it. It wasn't guaranteed to work but what else could I do? I could barge in pretending to be drunk? As I stood in the entryway, mind racing, the door to the street opened. I spun around and two large Russians shouldered in. Reinforcements.

The situation was out of control. My training kicked in. I didn't want to leave this American to his fate, but there was nothing I could do. We were outnumbered 5-to-2 with no plan in place. I finished my abrupt turn as smoothly as I could, stepped aside to let the blocky Russians through, and exited to the street. There were several street-facing windows, but heavy curtains blocked any view of the dining room inside. I strolled fretfully down the street, thinking the situation over but finding no solution. As I did, a single shot rang out in the night, and my heart sank. The sound came from the alley behind the restaurant. I shuddered at the immediacy of the execution, and at the fact that a few minute's time was the only thing that had separated me from sitting at the same table and suffered the same fate. I made my way back to the safehouse, but sleep that night was hard to find.

CHAPTER 8

Monaco

Life in the 10th SFG wasn't all life-and-death work. Like other divisions of the army, men of the 10th were entitled to stretches of leave and time away from the war. Every six months or so, I would exfiltrate from Berlin to either spend time traveling through Allied Europe or simply relax at an army base near a town that had plenty of pubs full of friendly people that could keep me occupied. It was a welcome break from the constant tension of operating in Berlin.

On one such leave, I traveled to Monaco with a fellow member of the 10th SFG. Together we explored the coastal city-state, enjoying the hot days and the temperate nights of the mediterranean climate. The soft white sand and turquoise waters of the world-famous beaches were unlike anything I had ever seen before, and the Belle Époque architecture of its famous buildings, like the Casino de Monte-Carlo and the Opéra de Monte-Carlo, was stunning.

We were far from the only Americans in the town, which was a common vacation destination for the wealthy. Over drinks at a bar near our hotel, I learned that hundreds of celebrities were all arriving to attend the wedding of Grace Kelly, the famous American actress, who was to wed the Prince of Monaco, Rainier III. The event was of international interest and scheduled for the following weekend. The reception was rumored to have an invitation list over 3000, and I immediately began fantasizing about attending the wedding. The only thing I could imagine being more fun than partying in Monaco would be partying in Monaco at an international royal wedding chock-full of celebrities. After thinking it over a bit, I turned to my vacation buddy and said, "Hey Ricky, I have an idea."

Ricky groaned. He knew my ideas were always trouble. "Oh ya, what's that, Tommy?"

"Let's infiltrate the reception-" Ricky barked a laugh, probably thinking - hoping - I was joking, but I quickly continued, "-it wouldn't be hard. We could rent one of those cars - you know, the fancy ones they all drive to this sort of thing. Then one of us plays chauffeur, we drive up, and boom! We're in."

"There is absolutely no way it's that easy." Ricky objected. "Surely they'll have invitations or something."

"What's the worst that can happen? They throw us out?" I replied, nudging him with an elbow. "And think of who we'll see if we get in. This is Grace Kelly getting married! I bet even Frank Sinatra will be there. Cmon, let's give it a shot."

Ricky wasn't optimistic about our chances, but in the end I wore him down, and he agreed. We went out and found a place where we could rent tuxedos, and then tracked down a car rental agency. But how to decide who would drive and who would ride along, role playing the celebrity? We agreed on a coin toss, which I won.

"Of course" Ricky grumbled as I slid smoothly into the back seat, grinning ear-to-ear. He had always been a sore loser. We drove off toward the Hotel de Paris where the post-ceremony wedding festivities were being held.

The approach up the winding driveway was lined by palm trees and perfectly manicured landscaping. As we turned the final corner, rolling into an oval loop, the enormous white hotel came into full view, covered in huge windows and ornate statues. Ricky pulled the car up to the front steps and I stepped out with confidence. He watched from the car in wonder as the doorman bowed deferentially and gestured upward toward the hotel entrance. I smiled and nodded, turning back toward the car to make a hidden celebratory gesture.

"The fool was right!" Ricky cursed under his breath and looped the car back around toward the parking area. From there he was able to sneak in a side entrance and hunt me down in the crowd of others assembling on the main floor. As he stepped up, I turned, gestured broadly and said with a smile, "Well, here we are!"

The gathering was an incredible sight. The event hadn't even started and I could pick out a few Hollywood folks I recognized: Cary Grant and Ava Gardner had walked by already. We threaded our way through the crowd and managed to acquire several hor'dourves from circling serving staff. The throng was so large that I was beginning to think we'd be able to stay all night so long as we kept to ourselves and didn't do anything too plebeian by accident.

Once we found the bar, we partook liberally of the cocktails. For over an hour we circled, sipped, and marveled at the wood paneling with golden inlays, the commanding portraits hanging on the walls, and the occasional celebrity citing. Aha - there was Gloria Swanson!

A bell rang and guests started collecting at an entrance leading to the dining hall. As I waited in line, I wondered what kind of hotel had a dining hall that could fit so many people. I couldn't wait to see all of the famous guests sitting and chatting together. But as we waited, I noticed that something was amiss: there was a doorman who appeared to be talking to each guest as they entered. How could we convince him of our rightful place at the reception dinner? The three cocktails I had enjoyed helped provide a series of compelling stories: I was Grace Kelly's cousin, serving in the U.S. Army in Monaco! I was the son of an old family friend! But as we got closer to the front of the queue, Ricky nudged me in the ribs and whispered, "They're checking invites!"

Sure enough, each new guest in line was being prompted to produce a finely lettered note. Perhaps the seating for dinner was arranged in advance and guests were being shown to their place. We looked at each other, nodded in unison, and ducked out of line and toward the main entrance. We stepped out easily into the cool April evening. As soon as we were far enough away, we both broke out into loud laughter. "Damn," I said, wiping tears from my eyes and trying to grimace disappointedly. "I'd wager a dollar they're serving lobster."

In truth, I knew we were lucky to have gone undetected for so long. Two military boys dressed in suits, mixing with celebrities. Who would believe it?

CHAPTER 9

The European Theater

The original operational goals of the 10th SFG were focused on infiltration behind the Iron Curtain in Berlin to stir up resistance to communism. However, our successes in the early 1950s led to an expanding sphere of influence. I began to go on missions that were further and further from the streets of Berlin.

One July, Russia moved border forces into the town of Fulda, in West Germany, several miles outside the Berlin city limits. The infraction was less than a hundred yards, and it was more of a case of Russia pretending the borders had changed rather than the beginning of an invasion. It was brazen, but striking back with military force would be seen as an escalation. I was tasked with making the Russian forces unwelcome - without starting a war.

Passing the border in the forest to the north of the Russian contingent was easy. The question was what - other than a bullet between the eyes - would make the Soviets reconsider their subtle advance? How could I send a message to their leadership that the Allies were watching and wouldn't tolerate similar aggression in the future? I knew just the thing.

Two other men volunteered to assist me, and as soon as it was dark, we crossed the border in a densely wooded area a mile north of our target. We crept south toward the Russian encampment, past the sentries, the ammunition piles, and the food supplies to arrive at a line of tanks parked in a clearing near the Russian tents. All we would need is a little mud, and it rained plenty in Germany in July.

It took only 15 minutes to pack the exhaust pipes of each of the half-dozen tanks completely full with mud from a nearby ditch. It was the perfect consistency, just wet enough to make it easy to stuff in, but dry enough that by morning it would be well set and impossible to clean out quickly. We were supposed to return during the same night, but I didn't want to miss the fun of watching a bunch of Russians scratch their heads at a backfiring tank. I was able to convince my two companions it would be worth it, so we huddled on a nearby hill to wait until morning. As light broke over the encampment, we watched through binoculars as the Russians milled about, the tanks shuddering to a halt a few seconds after each attempt to start them up. Whatever movements the invaders had planned for the day were ruined. We returned to West Germany happy with our success, and although it did take a few additional sabotage trips, the Russians conceded their ill-gotten slice of the forest border in less than a week.

I was also sent to Sweden many times, since I spoke fluent Swedish. Sweden's neutral status during World War II had established it as a black market of information and goods that both sides of the war had benefited from. Even though the war was over, Sweden continued to be a base for covert operations for both the Allies and the Soviets. In 1957, I was sent by boat to the Eastern shore of Sweden to investigate the feasibility of delivering agents behind enemy lines using motorboats in the Baltic Sea. The idea was to reverse engineer the Great Escape that my father had been a part of 13 years earlier. Instead of fleeing west from Estonia toward the safe haven of Sweden, the U.S. would deliver men directly to the Estonian coast where they could pass inland undetected to important targets. I was to travel to sea towns and identify boats and docks that we would be able to conscript. In order to make the trip quickly and avoid detection, we were primarily looking for newer models of motorboats. Their owners, of course, would need to be amenable and have no ties to communism.

Standing on a dock in the tiny marina of one such town, Vaxholm, I remember staring south across the Baltic toward Estonia. I felt frustrated. There I was, paving the way for a behind-enemy-lines mission to my homeland, a land I myself hadn't been back to for 12 years. I had hoped that by joining the U.S. military I would be able to go back home, but I had been in the army for three years by then and had still not been back to Estonia. My duty had returned me to Germany and Sweden, the places I had been a refugee, but there hadn't been a mission that sent me home. At least, not yet. I had gone from the Everglades of Florida to the forests of North Korea. I still had some hope that someday, surely, there would be an opportunity to go back to my homeland. In the meantime, since it was the base of our operations, I was coming to think of Berlin as my home.

The next time I received orders for an international mission, it was still not Estonia. Instead, it was for another return to Sweden, this time flying to the Bromma airport in Stockholm. In 1958 there were only three commercial airlines operating out of Berlin: British Airways, Air France, and Pan Am. I caught a direct Pan Am flight from Berlin to Bromma with one other member of the 10th SFG. Our goal was to monitor the Russian Embassy: the Army believed the Soviets were using it to smuggle covert agents in and out of Allied territory. After all, that's what we were doing. If the U.S. could do it, the Russians could do it too.

My fellow soldier and I rented a ground-floor apartment across the street from the Soviet Embassy and set up a traditional surveillance operation. We took turns, one watching while the other slept and ate. It was the most boring kind of operation you could be assigned, and I hated it. For three days we watched the embassy carefully, peering into each and every car that left the building. I grew more and more dissatisfied day by day as nothing happened. We hadn't found a single one of the agents we had been tasked with finding. Finally, on the fourth day, my patience wore out.

That night, I convinced my partner to haul our cameras up three flights of stairs to a top-floor apartment that looked down on the street. We had a worse view of the car drivers and passengers, but a much clearer view of the embassy's upper floors, and we could still watch the cars come and go. The next day, as I peered down onto the afternoon departure of a Russian vehicle, the reason we hadn't been able to spot any of the men we had been watching for became clear: there was a Russian lying on the floor of the back seat of the car, invisible from our observation spot three floors below. We had finally found our man! I reported the result to the U.S. Embassy in Stockholm, concluding the mission and finally ending the wait-and-watch misery.

In the end, though I operated in and around the Baltic Sea during my time in the 10th SFG, I never received the orders to return to Estonia. I learned, much later, that my research and reconnaissance in Sweden had actually been used to deliver another agent to work behind enemy lines in neighboring Latvia. As much as I longed to be sent on a mission to the area, I was fortunate to have avoided that particular assignment. The agent was caught shortly after landing and died in a firefight with Russian forces outside of Riga. Being passed over for this Latvian infiltration mission was one of many close calls during my time in the 10th SFG.

Another time, during a routine underground contact in Berlin, members of the 10th SFG learned that a group of Russian spies had been located in Munich, a day's train ride away. I was recruited to join for the mission to apprehend or eliminate the threat. It wasn't clear what the Russian spies' purpose was, but the sooner we could get there, the more likely it was that we could put a stop to it, and the less likely it was that the Russians would be able to disappear back into East Germany.

Three other members of the 10th joined me for the trip on the one train out of Berlin to Frankfurt, where we transferred to travel south to Munich. Even though Munich was in the American-controlled portion of the country, we had been ordered to travel undercover. It was likely there were Russian informants in the Allied Security forces and we knew for certain there were spies in the German *Bereitschaftspolizei*, or BePo, which had taken on a paramilitary security role in West Germany. Any news of our arrival in Munich from Berlin might spook the group we were after, so we traveled in secret. We would have no support from the friendly forces occupying Munich, but we weren't too concerned about that. This was how we often operated in Berlin, so Munich would be no different.

The intelligence report had been thorough, so we knew exactly where to begin looking for our targets. It took only one evening of checking bars and restaurants to find the group of spies in a small, one-room pub in the Schwabing district. The standard approach was to lie in wait outside the building, track the group to their safehouse, and eliminate them by catching them unawares during the night or as they came or went. But this tiny pub offered a uniquely efficient alternative: bombing the place would kill them all at once. The only problem was the civilians.

Joined by one other fellow, I entered the pub and nonchalantly ordered drinks. The Russians - a group of four - were sitting together in the back. A mix of full and half-drained vodka glasses covered the table in front of them. It was half-past 10 pm, and over the course of the next 15 minutes my fellow agent and I slowly worked our way around the room, discreetly warning all the other patrons that they should leave before 11 pm. The pub slowly emptied out, but we timed our disclosures so there was no mad rush for the door that might alert the Russians. There wasn't too much of a chance of that anyway, though, since they were busily adding to their table's glass collection.

At 11:00 pm sharp, I made my exit, noting approvingly that the bartender was doing the same. That did catch the Russian's attention, who suddenly looked around and found themselves in an empty room. "Now"! I shouted as I opened the door to the main street. One of our men was standing by, hand grenade ready. They pulled the pin, rolled the primed grenade into the room, and I slammed the door shut. There was a moment of loud cursing and then an explosion.

We had been so focused on clearing out the civilians before the assassination that we hadn't considered that some of them might call the police. As the grenade went off, I could hear the sirens of security police arriving to apprehend the bombers. We ran for it. It's possible that after being arrested we would have a chance to explain that we were American soldiers and the dead men were Russian agents. Counter-intelligence assassination and murder aren't the same thing in the eyes of the law. But we *had* just bombed a bar, and the police might not be keen to listen to our reasons for doing so. We didn't want to have to try to explain anything while staring at the wrong end of a pistol, and I definitely didn't want to spend the night on the floor of a German jail cell.

A few city blocks away we commandeered a vehicle and sped out of the city. Once in the suburbs, we ditched the car and found an abandoned farm where we could lay low until the search was called off. I found it ironic that we were forced into an evasion exercise deep in US-held territory, but that was the nature of being in the 10th SFG. Not even our own allies knew the extent of the shadowy war we waged. It was several days until we were able to safely return to the city center to catch a train back to headquarters in Berlin.

Tom Saar in uniform, age 26.
Virginia, 1960

CHAPTER 10

Exit Plan

Lodge Act recruits were offered a deal when we enlisted: 5 years of service in exchange for American citizenship. As 1959 came to a close, I was faced with a hard choice. Did I want to continue serving? I had participated in a new form of shadow war and helped establish the 10th SFG as an integral part of defending Berlin, preparing Germany for a Soviet invasion, and staving off nuclear war. By this time, we had begun to wear the green berets that would later become synonymous with the Special Forces. I had been an instrumental part of something special and felt like I had found both a family and a purpose.

But my time in the 10th SFG had taken a toll. I had personally killed dozens of Russians and had had several close calls like the one in Mannheim. I had watched my fellow soldiers die. Plus, I had met a woman from Sweden - Astrid - and we were to be married soon. While the 10th SFG was essential to fighting Russian influence in Europe, I knew it would take more than sabotage missions to free my homeland. It would take many years, if it ever came at all. I had done the required time, and there were others who could carry on the fight. After 5 strenuous and dangerous years, I decided I was done.

I had no idea what to do next. I informed the unit leadership that I did not intend to renew my contract, but I had no plan. I had been a shadow for the last 4 years, just a changing name and secret mission. I had only spent a few months in America, and the idea of starting a new life there at

26 years old was daunting. I had no idea where to go or what kind of work I would do instead. I could return to my parents in Sweden, but then I wouldn't be able to secure my American citizenship - one requirement was that I go to live in the United States. I wanted to leave the military, but I needed a cover story to ease my return to civilian life. Simply quitting and moving to the United States was out of the question - I was deeply concerned that the Russian intelligence agencies would be able to track my movements and determine that the Estonian who disappeared from Berlin was the same one who appeared in America. They might hunt me down after the fact.

First, I asked to be transferred out of the 10th SFG into a mundane supply role in America. It was a bittersweet change, as I had to say goodbye to Berlin, the place I had called home, and the men I had come to consider family. I was assigned to join the quartermaster post at Fort Lee in Virginia at the beginning of 1960. The work was a constant stream of paperwork, inventory and inspections - incredibly boring compared to the 10th SFG - but I knew it was best to wait until all the pieces were in place before making the final move. For 6 months I worked and settled into life in Petersburg, Virginia. During those months, I got a surprise call. I was invited to travel to Washington D.C. to be part of a citizenship ceremony! The paperwork for my American citizenship had been approved. I hadn't even applied yet, thinking that I would do so after starting my civilian life. Fortunately, the Army had taken care of everything on my behalf. I made the 2 hour drive from Petersburg to Washington and - in the shadow of the U.S. Capitol - took the oath that sealed my status as a citizen.

With my citizenship attained, there was no barrier to finding a civilian job. I knew a few ex-Army men who had settled in Boston, so I contacted them. Nothing was guaranteed, but they assured me work would be available if I moved there. Boston had a climate more similar to Estonia and Sweden than Virginia. It was near the ocean like Tallinn, and it had the same long winters and springs that I had grown accustomed to in

Stockholm. Besides, it was May, and I already yearned for some relief from the increasingly warm Virginia summer. Army policy would allow me to rejoin without any loss of rank if I had left service less than six months ago, so I figured I could use that time to move north and see how I liked it. If it didn't work out, I could reenlist. In June of 1960, I was honorably discharged from the U.S Army after 5 and a half years of active duty. I was able to find work in Massachusetts, and I still live in New England 63 years later.

I often think back to this final decision as a soldier. Had my move to Boston fallen flat, I may have reenlisted and rejoined the fight in Berlin. Then again, if any of my missions behind enemy lines had gone differently, I might never have made it to America at all. And if my parents hadn't fled Estonia in 1941, I might have met my end in a Siberian labor camp. Instead, I was fortunate to play a small part in the Cold War fight to free Estonia, like my Uncle Paul had in WWII.

Though Estonia was still firmly in Russian hands when I moved to America, I had exacted a measure of revenge. The fire I felt for avenging my homeland had cooled, but smoldered on in my chest throughout the 1960s, 70s, and 80s. Then, after the fall of the Iron Curtain, I returned to Estonia in the 1990s. I had spent 50 years - an entire lifetime - as a refugee. On my return visit I reclaimed my family farm and learned the fate of grandmother and my Uncles, Paul and Fritz. Estonia had spent most of the 1900s occupied by Russia, but at last it was free. And so was I.

Tom and his wife, Astrid, after Tom received his U.S.
citizenship.
Virginia, 1960

I was in the back of the car lot when the call came. "Hey Tom, there's a customer up here, wants to take a ride with you!"

"What? Isn't John on the floor today? Have him ride with John." I called back. I had no idea why a customer would want to test drive a car with me. In the year since moving here, I had developed a reputation as the kind of direct, hard-working car salesman that was easy to talk business with. I didn't sugarcoat the bad stuff, though I did have a knack for redirecting the conversation to the benefits a particular vehicle might provide. But this was something all the salesmen did, and I wasn't anyone special in Brockton, Massachusssets.

A few minutes later another shout came. "He wants you, Tom". Frowning to myself, I turned and slowly walked toward the main building that held the dealership offices.

Inside, a tall middle-aged man waited for me, staring out the front windows toward the road. As he turned, a smile broke across his angular face, but there was no friendly warmth in it. His eyes were cold and hard. I didn't recognize him, and I didn't like the look of him. "Hi Tom," the stranger said, reaching out to shake my hand in greeting. "Let's go for a ride."

Wary but willing, I followed the man as he turned and walked toward an unremarkable 5-year old Chevy Bel Air. He slid into the driver's seat and I walked around and got in on the other side, turning to look at this strange-mannered man. At first, the customer was silent, seeming to listen intently to the rumble of the engine as he started the car. He pulled out of the dealership and down the sunny Massachusetts road. The silence was tense, but I waited. After a few minutes, the man started listing names.

Paul. Gerte. Fritz. Helene. The hair on the back of my neck stood up as I heard the names of my family members fall out of the driver's mouth. I hadn't seen any of them since fleeing Estonia as a child. Today, that part of the world was locked away behind the Iron Curtain. This fellow must be Russian Intelligence… and that means he knew who I was. I stayed calm; I was trained for situations like this.

"They're all living happily where they want to be," The strange man said. "You could be too. You'd be welcomed home with open arms."

Home. It was a place I thought about often, though I wasn't sure I would ever be able to return. Images of riding my horse and hunting trips with the family dogs flashed through my memory and I eyed the man driving the car, thinking carefully about how to reply.

Before I could, the agent proceeded to outline an offer. I could return to Estonia and join the Soviet intelligence agency. My knowledge of the Allied special forces would be highly valued and I would be provided a lifestyle to match. Behind the Iron Curtain I'd be safe, comfortable, near family, and there would be no need to peddle used cars.

"I'll give you 14 days to think it over." Sensing my hesitation, the driver let the car coast and paused thoughtfully. "It would be best if this conversation stayed between us. Tell anyone, and I'll have to pay a visit to your beautiful new wife. I know how she likes to bathe every day… I'd have to stop by at an inopportune time. It would be such a shame if she electrocuted herself in the bathtub." I didn't honor the threat with a reply, and the remainder of the ride was silent.

I always knew my past could chase me into civilian life, but it was terrifying to have a visit from Soviet intelligence less than a year after my discharge from the United States Army. I had intentionally transferred out of the 10th Special Forces Group before leaving the service, becoming a member of the quartermaster post at Fort Lee in Virginia. By spending the final days of my service in an unremarkable position, I had hoped to build a cover story for the 5 years I had spent in the 10th. Tom from the quartermaster's unit was a replacement for Tom the spy behind enemy lines. An ineffectual replacement, apparently.

At 27 years old and with less than a year in America under my belt, I did not have many good options. That night I discussed those options with my wife, Astrid. We agreed - despite the risks - to contact law enforcement. The next morning I called Frank, a friend from my time in the Army who now worked at the Boston office of the Federal Bureau of Investigation.

I met with Frank the next day at a diner several towns away. I needed to keep a low profile, thanks to the threats from the Russian. I recounted the strange car customer's visit, from start to finish. Frank nodded along nonchalantly while eating a large portion of eggs. I was too tense to eat, sticking with a cup of black coffee. Finally, Frank took out a notepad and jotted down a description of the Soviet agent as well as the license plate that I had memorized as the fellow drove away. Frank assured me between sips of his own coffee that the FBI would "take care of it". He refused to elaborate beyond that. It was going to be a long two weeks until the Russian's deadline.

I went straight from the diner to the store and bought a gun. Then I went home and Astrid, "if anyone knocks while I'm out, just shoot through the goddamn door. Don't even ask any questions. Just shoot."

But Astrid had never shot a gun before, so I set up a target in the basement and taught her the basics. Use the safety, steady your aim, and be ready for the recoil. It was exactly the sort of thing I had hoped to avoid when I retired my green beret, but I didn't see another way to keep her safe. Laying in bed that night, I kept replaying the car conversation over and over in my mind, haunted by the chilling tone in the man's voice when he talked about electrocuting her. Somehow it was different when the threat was toward her.

With a bit of coaxing and reassurance, I had her firing confidently enough in just a few days. Knowing Astrid would at least have a chance to defend herself allayed some of my concerns, but not all. Word from Frank couldn't come soon enough.

I kept working at the car dealership, though I told the front desk fellow to kick out the Russian if he showed his face. But he never did, even after the two weeks passed. Eventually I inquired with Frank about what had happened, but there was no reply. Every day I returned home from work with a knot of dread in my stomach, and every day Astrid was there, safe. Two weeks turned into two months, and slowly the cloud of anxiety hanging over our life dissipated.

One day 6 months later, we got a surprise invitation from Frank. He was hosting a St. Patrick's day party at his house down on Cape Cod. Together, Astrid and I formulated a plan: since my inquiries had been rebuffed many times, she would ask. After the evening's festivities were well underway and Frank had gotten nice and drunk, she'd dance with him and slip in the question.

When she did, Frank gave her an incredulous look and laughed brazenly. "Oh, that guy?!" Leaning in so only she could hear, he reassured her, "He's no more honey, you got nothing to worry about."

The End

APPENDIX

Tom's mother, Leida, poses next to German soldiers in Berlin.
Germany, 1941

Tom, age 7, strikes a pose with his mother on the streets of
Berlin.
Germany, 1941

Tom (middle), his mother Leida (left) and his uncle Fritz
(right) in Berlin, waiting out the first Russian occupation of
Estonia.
Germany, 1941

A sign remembering the Tallinn bombing on March 9, 1944.
Tallinn, Unknown

Made in the USA
Middletown, DE
08 June 2023